1

het jaar 2022
the year 2022

a small catalogue of thoughts
on healing and heartache
while traveling

by sabina petra

4

Book Cover by Sabina Petra / Photographs by Sabina Petra

1st edition 2025

ISBN 979-8-9926389-0-5

1. lente (spring)          thirteen poems

2. zomer (summer)          eleven poems

3. herfst (autumn)         eleven poems

4. winter                  sixteen poems

# 1. lente (spring)

## london

**one.**

what if you could never recognize someone
by their faces?
what if they could change bodies everyday like clothes
or have it handed to them like uniforms
and you could only recognize someone by the cock of their head
the glint in their eye
the crack of their joke?
you'd have to look at people so much more closely

**two.**

i cannot sleep for wanting
for wanting a voice, a stage, a reach, a chance
for wanting your voice, your eyes, your focus, your hands,
one on my face and one on my hips
i walk around furiously dreaming
i cannot sleep for wanting
to live instead of sleeping

**three.**

i am a successful human being
i can carry an intelligent conversation
i have learned a lot
and am always willing to learn more
i write stories where there were once only
empty pages
i am a good listener, a sensitive speaker
i am passionate and hardworking
an honest person
i have many ideas and questions
actively marvel at the world and the universe
i believe in the good of people
in the power of love
and i am a very decent kisser

but i am poor and therefore i have failed
the shame surrounding it blocks the light
from all the immaterial things i've accomplished
it casts a huge shadow
because for as long as i can remember
i have been taught what responsibility looks like;
> hard work
> equals
> good pay
> results in
> a worthy human being
anyone who's not financially viable
is either lazy
or a failure
and can't get their life together

my father holds money in such high esteem
that if i would ask for some
i might as well be asking for a kidney
this kidney would be talked about in every circle of my family
sabina got a kidney from her dad
he is the best father in the world
sabina's body is a freeloader
coasting about on another person's kidney
that kidney was hard earned and now she's enjoying it

never mind that words can start a heart
you could lose a kidney
not ideal but you could
you cannot lose a heart

i am a successful human being
but what constitutes success
and who gets to decide the definition?

**four.**

why do i feel like i've aged 5 years in 3 months?
my face has lines it never knew before
as if it's drawing a map of the world on my skin
roads and lakes and mountain ranges
will i ever be as smooth as the dunes in the sahara
beckoning lovers with mirages and rippling heat?
now all i'll attract are seasoned hikers
who like to scramble up granite
and camp amongst scraggly bushes

**five.**

masturbation is an odd thing
to imagine something pleasurable that isn't there
in order to get to a goal that is so fluttering and fleeting
a feeling that can't be defined as pure delight
more like a slightly transcendent pain
a portion of a second of ecstasy
and after that mere portion of a second
i'm left more hollow than before
missing the skin i was imagining
realizing the build up was the best part
not the goal

**six.**

as soon as i have found myself,
i am looking for myself again
this enrages me:
if i have befriended myself,
i should be able to hold on to her at all times

but our own friendship can be as slippery as any other
we are mercurial beings,
changing temperature and shape
made out of water, malleable
altered every moment

one day is not like the next
some days i have planted my roots,
on others i am like a leaf in the wind
if i want to be my own friend,
i have to figure out anew
what element i'm in

**seven.**

they say pain is there to teach us
but
what is it teaching me now?
what is the lesson of it staying for so long?
why does it linger
or rather
why does it have a tide
ebb and flow
here and not
healed and back to broken?

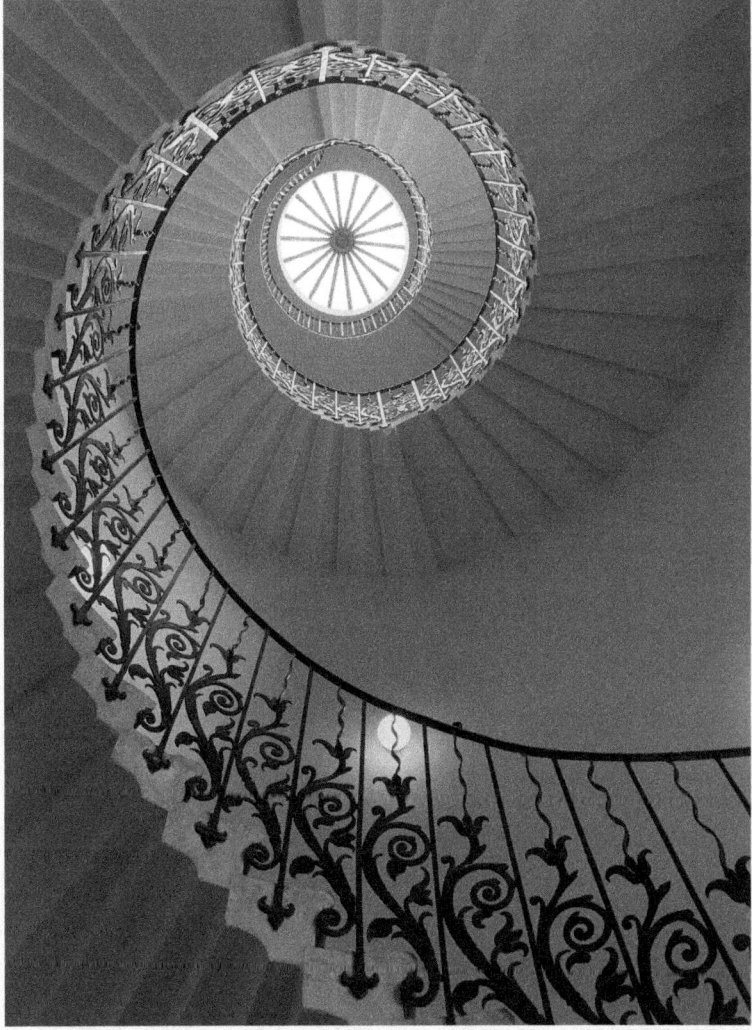

**eight.**

i put my forehead to your collarbone
then slowly
simply, warmly
kiss the space just beneath your jaw
so soft there
you linger your lips above my eye
you kiss it ever so lightly
then you hover above my lips
you kiss lightly again
again
again
there is something heartbreakingly passionate about something
so light

**nine.**

how are some days so full
so exciting
beautiful
you bask in the glory, the warmth of your life

and then there are others where
the day seems utterly empty
no matter what you do or how hard you work
time slips through your fingers and you wonder
why you lived this day at all
and who knows whether you are, in fact, alive
where the past is as tangible in your mind as the present
and the future as unforgivingly vague as this moment
suspended in worry about who to be

today was the latter
i hope tomorrow is the first

**ten.**

apart from the ornamental ceiling
adorned with flowers, shells and cherubs
some gold leaf in the front of the church
there are no likenesses
no altars, no candles
no paintings or idols
it is merely this great hull of a ship
vast, curved, with lots of windows
to hold us all together while we sail across life
this is where a greater thing is worshipped;
a spirit within us;
community
and it scares me,
because of late community has felt very frail

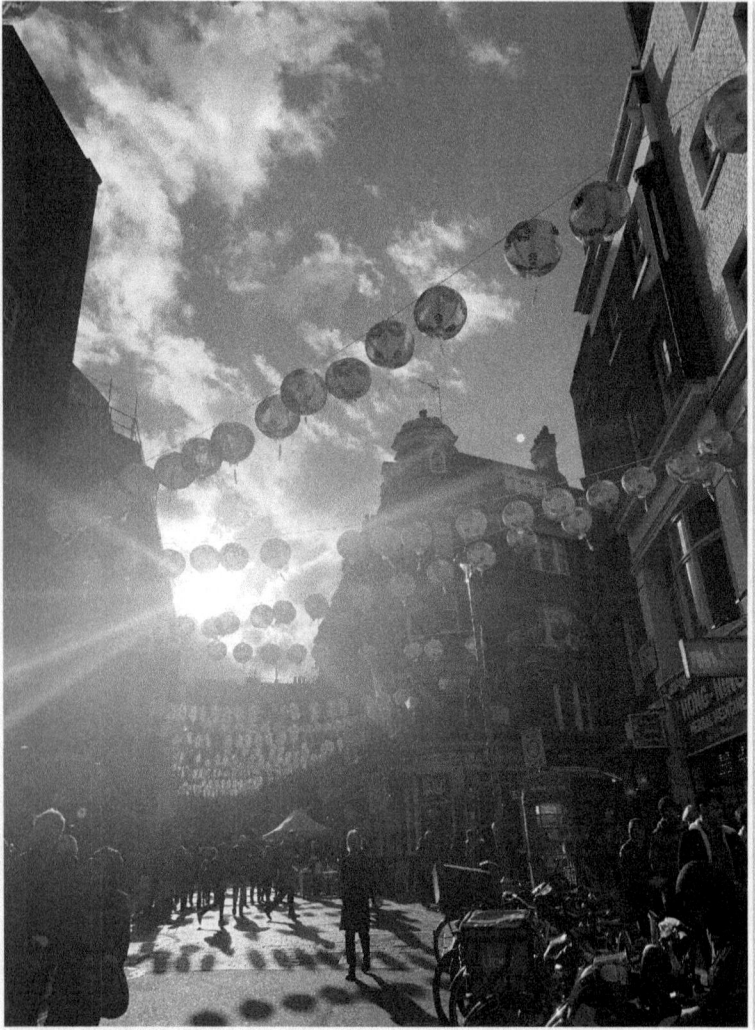

**eleven.**

i love love
i have been born with the love for love
it has come from a long line of lives lived, loving love

i don't understand how i have not been able to secure love
to be sure of love, to have it as the sturdy pillar of my existence

i have chased it
i have seen it, wanted it, gone for it
it has beckoned me
it has said:
       here i am, ripe for the plucking
i took my basket and scrambled up the ladder
and shook that tree dry
only to find it bore one fruit
not hundreds, as i had thought

i have not stopped wanting love
i will want love and want want for all my wandering years
i have simply
adjusted my conditions;
i don't want anything fleeting
i don't want anything that doesn't fight for me
that doesn't run to me, arms full of fruit

**twelve.**

i can't seem to find my own balance today
i've tripped many times,
either over pavement stones,
or my own ankles
either over a couple of percentages of alcohol,
or my own thoughts
it made me realize
i look for stability outside of myself so often

breathe, sabina, breathe
find your equilibrium again

**thirteen.**

when i felt my world crumbling around me
i was convinced there was no way out
the pain was indescribable
there were no words for it, only shards
a broken body, a shattered soul
my brain couldn't coil its coils around a solution
this was my life
it was going to be my life
forever

even though i remember thinking
i was never going to come up for air
i don't remember the drowning
even though i remember i was breaking
that it felt never-ending
i don't remember the pain

it will come again
and again
you will give birth
to the next era
again
and again
and it will still be painful
it will still be horrible
but afterwards you will hold a new life
in your hands
and the pain will be forgotten

because here i am
and i don't remember

**2. zomer (summer)**

**new york, ny**
**lynchburg, va**

**one.**

i made a mistake
i wrote;
2922
not;
2022

funny how it immediately triggers an image
can you imagine?
2922
almost the end of the millennium
900 years from now
it's almost unfathomable
it is unfathomable
nothing almost about it

what would we have
what would we not?

interplanetary travel?
space cars in our back yard?

did animals and plant life evolve?
do they rule the world?

do we still see each other
make contact?
did we go back into caves,
painting on walls?

did we destroy everything
build beautiful structures
contacted other life forms
extinguish our own?

am i there?
do i love you?

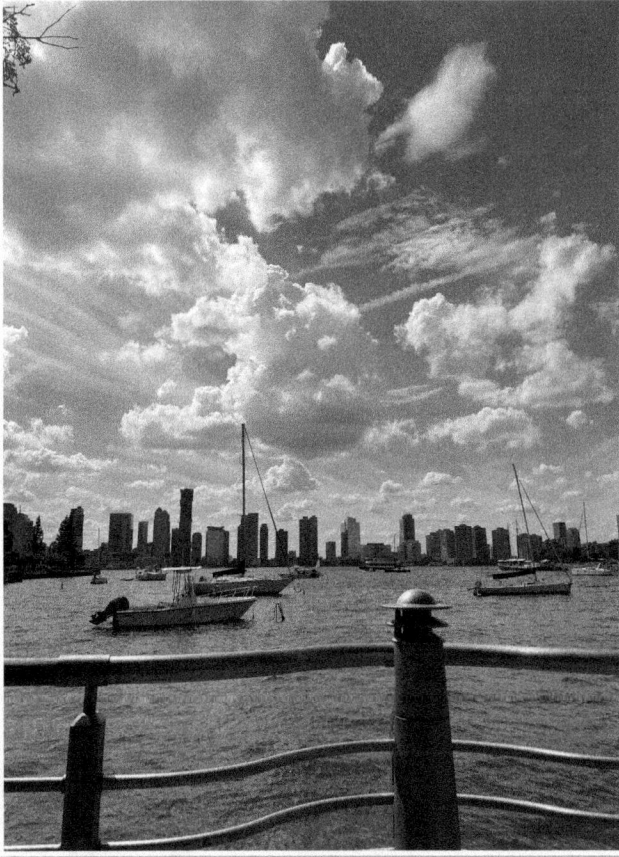

**two.**

we've been through a lot together
i recognize you
recognition is not the same as love
even though it can fool you

**three.**

beauty is a question of bearing
isn't it?
of pulling your shoulders down,
putting your heart out, your nose in the air

of being tall instead of short,
broad instead of small,
of taking up space

beauty is essentially the way you carry yourself,
and the opinion will follow

**four.**

i want to cry
over everything we weren't able to become
but instead i'm crying
for what all others were

how is it i get more involved
with other stories
mostly fake ones
televised ones
than my own
or the news?

i always want another heart
yours
yours and yours and yours
always out of reach
and too open to be real
real life is less
purposeful
and takes more
guts

that's why i'm so harsh and hard
i have a soft heart but its guarded
by lots of guts

**five.**

the old adage is true
i learned from example

from my father
i learned how to be quiet
i learned how to be logical
i learned to shut down
i learned how to be an adult before the age of 10

from my ex
i learned what men expect from a woman
how deep patriarchy lives
how to wear lingerie when i didn't feel like it
how to wear heels and deal with blisters

from theatre
i learned that magic is real
that people look different
and look at things differently
but what they say and what they do matters
more
than what they look like or think of
that i was wrong
and that many people could be wrong,
and still are beautiful

from travel i learned
that loneliness is different from solitude
that the earth knows more than we do
but the universe is a sniggering mystery
that energy courses through us,
connecting us
that it is real
that hiding and pondering are not the same thing

from a television series character
i learned that any age at all is a good age
to discover things about yourself
that everyone is a shade of (non) binary
that the way he walks and the way he tips his head upward
make me see the world from a better vantage point
that his joy and honesty means freedom

i've learned from example
i hope to teach by example too
i hope to teach things i haven't even seen anywhere else
something my body has always known
inherited knowledge
newly welled

how to live art
how to be a movie
how to love an idea, or a mind

in any case
it started with example
and in that way
a television series character
saved my life

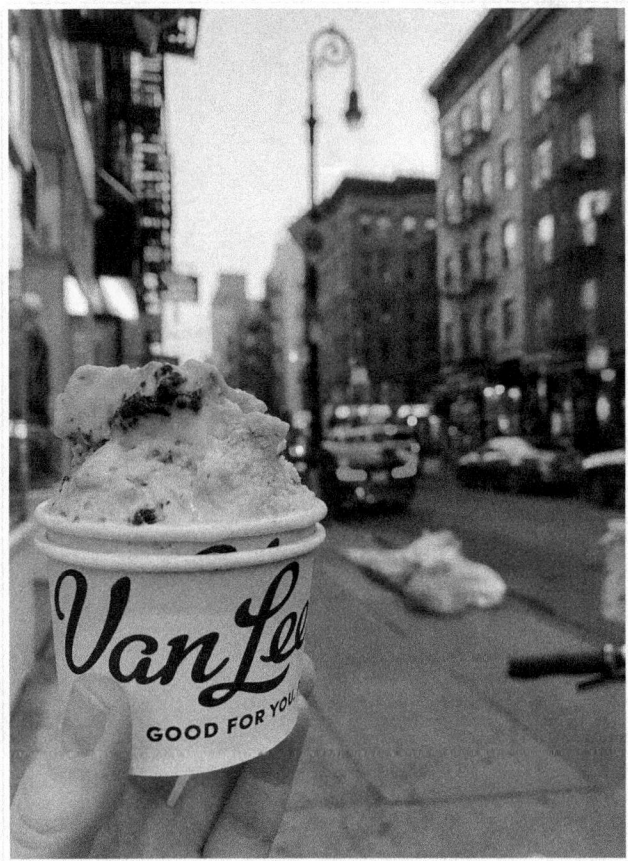

**six.**

i daydream so much
i am kind of proud of it
it is how my mind processes
stories, interest in humanity,
imagination, possibility
hope for love and connection

but i forget about the life i'm living
and i have so much going on
three shows and
two auditions and
an upcoming job
but somehow
all my minutes and hours
all my moods and prayers
go out to an image that exists
only in my mind
completely intangible
yet my whole body responds as it being solid earth

**seven.**

i enjoy being my own person
i enjoy the shape of my body
the make-up and the outfits
my long hair, my bright eyes

i like men
i like their firmness
their blunt excited goal searching
i like their strength and their height
i like the way their muscles move under their skin

i like you
you're so cute
you remind me of my primary school crush
he had freckles like you
and a mop of floppy hair just like yours
only darker
he had bright, sweet eyes
and dimples
your face is a little rounder
a little less guarded
you're so easy to like
or
easy to be like

your swagger and your reasoning
i want the swoop of your hair and the freckles
i want the pecs and the strong arms and the
big sweater and the vans
because somehow
it imbibes me with the strength of
your gender
your intention

your open heart
and your good luck

in male-driven stories
they fight like me
their willpower is like mine
their love is the same
when they do love
they fear like me
and desire like me
i sing male songs
perform male monologues
i took cyrano and made him a woman
in body only
because
the mind stays the same
the fight stays the same

i forget i am a woman sometimes
i don't get it when doors are closed to me
neighborhoods are considered unsafe
that i have to text when i get home
why?
i don't get hollered at on the street
i think they somehow understand
yet they don't know what to do with it

why does it make things more complicated instead of clearer?
all the heroes i wanted to play as a kid
all the adventures i wanted to live
i am trying to live them in a female body
in a male world
in a non binary mind

**eight.**

the coconut
probably from someone's hair
coffee and hay
the heat from the tarmac
the sun on my face
the residual warmth from the summer day
the sky a blue expanse
simple
friendly
unending
the wind in my hair
the green on the palate
these are the moments when i have no focus and no thoughts
a simple happiness of seeing life flash by as the car races
through the countryside

43

**nine.**

i could cry
i feel the salt crumbling from the caves within
for all the heart rending,
soul soaring things i've seen
for all the blooming,
windswept feelings i feel now
for all the crushing and
elated things to come

**ten.**

We are all sitting at a pool in a beautiful backyard. Maybe the Californian mountains are behind me. Palm trees shading the entrance gate. I don't know anyone here by face, and yet I know everyone by heart - we've been here for a while. We're all prisoners. We're in this together.

There is an announcement. We don't have to do any more daily sacrifices. The mandate in America has been lifted. Everyone is free, only 2 more days of "cull the population" exterminations.

Everyone leaves, but for a couple, another man, and me. We sit at the pool in the setting sun, and wait.
One half of the couple gets chosen. He disappears into dust, wafts into the air like nothing, like smoke. The other half wails, and leaves through the ornate iron gate.

It's just me and the other man. We are allowed to leave, and we will get a notification later today of who will be the last sacrifice. My dad is waiting to pick me up. I load my small pack of luggage into his convertible. It's basically a garbage bag filled with a diary, my favorite pens, my sunglasses, and an old cardigan.

We drive into the sunset, along the Pacific coast. We stop at a beach, where my dad walks a little ahead of me while I unload my belongings from the garbage bag onto the sand. He doesn't wait. I feel my phone vibrate. It's a very short message.
       It's you.

I call out to my dad, telling him that I was the one chosen for the last sacrifice. He doesn't want to come closer, he is washing his hands of me right there and then. Take care of my things, I ask him, implore him, and he answers; No no, that's your own responsibility, as he raises his hands and backs away in the soft sand, the Pacific rushing a song in our ears.

I feel a sharp pain shoot through my body, and suddenly I lift up, I lift into the sky and I am no more. My body breaks apart in the tiniest particles of sand, and becomes part of the beach. My soul drifts like a leaf in the wind across the coast, down onto the soft surface. I am aware that I am still aware, but cannot figure out what exactly I am now.

I wake up.

**eleven.**

am i pushing forth
with the life i was given
or was this the life
i wanted all along?

## 3. herfst (autumn)

**lynchburg, va**
**singapore**
**kuala lumpur**

**one.**

life is so joyful
and so dramatic
it flips in an instant
it's excruciating

but i'd rather feel everything
than nothing at all

**two.**

we kissed
because we had to
the moment choreographed
determined for us
a closed-mouthed affair

you had your hand on my face
your thumb tracing my jawline
back and forth
i had my fingers in your hair
the nape of your neck, where it swirls
your other hand curling around my waist
and i kissed you

and in that tiny gap
the truth can seep through
the heart can take a step inside
a flash of your memories leapt through my brain
and suddenly
a tiny confession
a concession

     i would love

if only
we'd live in this world
which we don't

oh my god
i can't stand you in the world we actually live in
but boy do i love you
utterly and completely
and so easily
in the world we don't

**three.**

the only reason for this sorrow
is the beauty that came before
but sorrow it is

**four.**

lady macbeth memories:

my scottish home
you
you and the memories of urquhart
the cold of the water and the small rowing boat we sailed off with
the stars we watched the whiskey we shared the blanket we huddled
under
the apples we took from the kitchen
the back of the castle where we stole our kiss
in the fierce last sunlight bouncing off the waves of the loch

our feet in the broken glass of the water
waving to people small as pinpricks from the other bank
looking at salmon colored skies
holding hands
singing by the fire, our friend our brother our confidant on the lute
dancing, slow to fast, fast to slow
burying my face in your neck
scraping my cheek against your scruff

your kisses your mouth your warmth
at the cairns, pressing our bodies together like they could fuse
our picnic discarded
in the halls of dunsinane
behind the curtain at the alcove
a barrier between the clothed and the unclothed world
between a world of sleep and a world of all senses awake
in the small loch on the mountain towards ben lomond
your freckled skin your arms like pillars of a cathedral over me
your chest the vaulted ceiling
your hair glowing strawberry in the sun
the wind caressing us but never chilling

your face in full rapture
my skin glowing white against the heather
my sighs lost to the clouds

home home
the fires and the smoke
the dances and the feasts and the time you talked about the horses flying
off the tapestries
so young so old so young
the dark wood the smell the mulch the trees
the whisky the bread the fruit the hot potatoes with butter and salt the
oat cakes
your hand always in mine your smile your reassuring gaze your bright
blue eyes
your honest laugh when i make a loud obscene remark
your crinkled face your back bent back in mirth
your kisses your mouth your warmth
your tears when we marry your tears when i comfort you your tears
when we lose our child
the heath the bog where we buried him
the wind carrying my song the ground absorbing your sobs
your kindness your honor your ease your charm

the heather the colors the ever-green and gold and rusty red the purple
the dark of the loch at night the cold the furs the heavy clothing the
stars the planets
the mulled wine the hearth the wild the old gods the mystical the blue
paint of my mother her necklace my first tattoos
when i got stolen out of my bed when i got forced to do unspeakable
things when i saw you out of the window when you got your first slash
across your face and the next time i saw you it was a blue tattoo i have
mine across my eye

my scottish home
is you and i, mourning loving lusting laughing crying

it is you and i, far apart and always so close in heart inseparable
two magnets bound to fuse together blast collide explode form
something new

i know you remember
i know you glance it sometimes
when you think back like i do
how it has become, somehow
ancestrally rooted within us as a truth
a story we actually lived
over and over

our home

and every so often
our hearts collapse in our chest
from missing it

**five.**

oof
you really fit together
love sports
military backgrounds
so ruddily, jovially southern
bright eyed, bushy tailed
old fashioned values
don't like to talk about painful pasts at all
having a body stocked with it
jeez
good luck

**six.**

a broken heart
cracks through the body
and into the day

it cracks the faces of people around you
it cracks the items in your hand
it cracks the words on your tongue
the sound in your ears
the food in your mouth

it cracks a line straight through the sky
through the light of the sun
through the time of the day
so that it stands still
at the time of your breaking

for everyone else
life seems as smooth as a stone milled by water
they don't understand the tears constantly seeping
through the cracks of your broken heart

**seven.**

  you're the best
  he says
  and he means it

i fall apart
in shards of paper
too light to fall to earth
scattering all over the world
all the places i've been
all the places i yet want to go

not like glass
sharp and colorful
not like stone
heavy and decisive
but soft and fluttering
landing on grass and in streams and on gusts of wind
disappearing in the landscape
carrying my words
words of hope
and love
and loyalty
of creation
melting into the dew of the morning

i've written:
  you're the best
  he says
  and i fall apart

because it's not me he says that to
no one says that
who can say that to me
and make me believe it?

because i've heard it
it's either not been true
or i couldn't accept it
i wanted to but
it had thorns,
those pretty petal words

how have i become this lost?
after all these journeys i've taken
how have i not found a hearth?

i want to go to the highlands
i want to go home
but i know that once i am there
the heather will whisper at me
the mountains will chuckle at me
under the breath of the brooks i will hear:
where have you gone?
once a queen, why are you a slip of paper?

**eight.**

i want to stop talking about you
or thinking
or writing

i want to think about me
i don't even want to talk or write
i want to think
and then do

there are so many beautiful things to come
there are so many beautiful things happening right now
and i don't want to miss them because of spending time
on an idea of you
when i know the solid facts
of me

i want to take a step forward
and another
i want to run
i want to do

가고 싶어
하자

**nine.**

i thought i had a good grip on
the boundaries of reality
yet somehow i still tie myself in knots over
my territory
terrified that someone might leave
or even think the slightest bit worse of me
as if it matters
as if i become a different person along with their opinion
quantum emotion;
      when observed, it changes
as if my intentions have shifted
and my work is shoddy
no way
when my every effort goes towards kindness

as if i suddenly wouldn't know who i am
when they change their minds
as if i'd lose everyone
as if i own anyone now

how can it still inform every action
that deep-seared trauma
when it really shouldn't

i don't own shit
only my own opinion
my own voice and thoughts
which should not be spent
on you

**ten.**

i always loved the nights the best
burying my face in your crewneck sweater
in the winter
or cradling my cheek between your shoulder blades
in the summer
inhaling the salt of your skin
your powerful arms surrounding me
not only a haven but a stronghold
a fleet of viking ships could attack and i would be
unharmed
protected by your sheer will of heart

i hate the nights the most
sleep is a strange jungle i wade through
to get to the other side where the day is like
a watering hole of some kind
with a little waterfall that casts rainbows on the wet stones
a slight breeze ruffles my hair
it is nice
but i always hold my machete close
for when the night comes

it saddens me to think
how easy it is to lose a stronghold
and be left with a machete

**eleven.**

i bought some scotch
in the state of virginia
and suddenly i feel at home
in two continents at once

it'll keep on going like this
the more countries i visit
the more people i meet
the more food i eat
the more i learn
the more i love
the more i'll miss

the more i will be home nowhere / everywhere

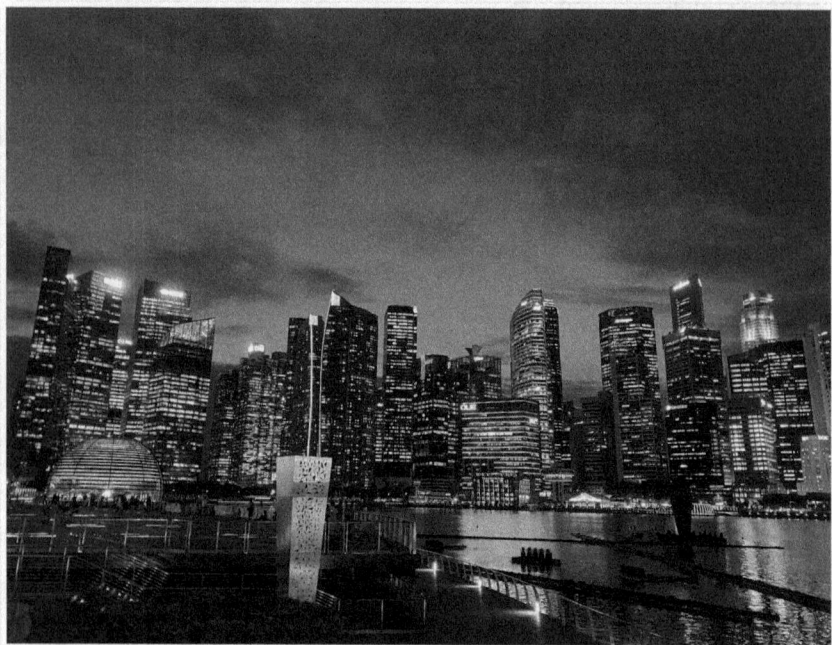

## 4. winter

**amsterdam / koog aan de zaan**
**isle of skye**
**cromarty**
**ben lomond**
**callandar**
**edinburgh**
**leeds**

**one.**

scotland is stripped
rugged, wild, harsh and lush
soft moss and jagged boulders
saturated colors of gold, rust and the deepest green

scotland is kin
she isn't the nicest
but she is truthful
wind whipping around my face
the cold seeping into my bones
as the clouds emptied from rain take my breath away
rays of sun tickle my cheeks
the art of making things cozy is a part of the culture
ever since the days of castles

we are both clear as day
this country and i
and have so many mysteries to reveal
so much treasure to uproot
the air crystal and the fog deep
icy diamond water and warming whiskey running through our veins

she knows you best whether you like it or not
shows you the worst parts of yourself and
challenges you to be better
scotland is kin
we understand each other
this stripped land and my stripped soul

**two.**

i just said goodbye to my mother
she knew it
she was crying - but holding it in
has to be strong, you see
has to keep up the armor
the skin has become chainmail
looks are daggers
words are ninja stars

our conversations are a jousting game
attack, defend, stab, turn the horse
attack again
we are supposed to
make each other feel loved and carried
what are we doing?

i didn't come back to give you grief
or to give you joy
i simply came back
we could've taken care of one another
instead we drowned ourselves in expectations
and chainmail is heavy
we sink fast

i feel guilty
there must be something i am not seeing
some gross mistake i have been making
how dare i skim over the smooth ice;
all the things my parents have given me
and stumble over the small cracks
of their doubts
translated into cold demeanors?
but again i tumble into the freezing water

of thinking i owe them something
so i yank my skates off

her face is a mask of pain
my heart is breaking
i'm so sorry mamma
i wish i were the girl you asked for
but i am not
and i am very tired of pretending to be
i've carried you all this way
if i don't ask for you to carry me
would it be alright if i just traveled without luggage for a while?

**three.**

you went into debt
only to lose the money
now you want to buy a car
and go into more debt

we're on the phone
i'm quiet for a moment
you chuckle

you say;
        you're like; what the fuck is he doing?

i smile;
        i'm not saying anything
        i'm making a face but
        i'm not saying anything

you laugh;
        i can tell

i wonder what you call that
when you can tell someone is
making a face over the phone

family?

**four.**

from here
it just seems like a silly game
a fully immersive video experience

while i get to see the planet
the beauty and reality of it
the whipping wind still stinging my face
stretching the skin across my cheeks
some weirdos in offices are deciding they want more power or land
that they're right and others are wrong

they look pasty and unhappy
in their starched cameo suits
they've been in the game too long
why don't they take a walk in the hills
look at the light of the sun playing games with the ocean
maybe they'd calm down and see sense

**five.**

will he ever see
how precious it was
how beautiful
how good it was what we had?

will he ever miss it?
will he ever find a pocket of time where
the stream of air will be cut off from his lungs
the pipe closed
and he will find
the world empty?

will he ever curse himself for
not understanding what he was holding in his very hands at the time?

or will life just flow through him
never thinking beyond the moment he's in
blissfully unaware of how much i loved him?

**six.**

you can only feel safe and warm
when you have been cold and in danger
or
at least be able to recognize the difference

a few days ago i stepped into a river
i didn't want to walk all the way back around it
and i had to get to the other side
it's rainy season in scotland so
the current is strong
a waterfall a mere 10 yards down
i cannot see how deep the river is
not too deep, right?
it is about 10 yards wide
and the stones are slippery
no way i'm getting across this without getting wet
but i know i've already made my decision
to go through it
not around
through the river
not around
through life
not around
come on river
come on stones
give me buoyancy
get me to the other side safely

i take one step
i calculated
it should come up to my calf
but the current takes my foot and sweeps it into a patch much deeper
in one fell swoop i'm up to my nipples in ice cold water

i take a deep breath in
the water is made of frozen needles but i am not cold
the breath is not one of shock
it is one of necessity
later i learned it was to make myself float
i vaguely realize i am banging my legs against sharp edges
and that i am moving towards the waterfall
with two mittened hands i grab a rock in the middle of the river
and swing myself around it upstream
i smack myself into the mud of the other bank
immediately i take out my phone and check if it's still working
thank god, it is
first things first, right?
then i laugh
haha stupid sabina
fell into a river
what an idiot
i look like a drowned cat
i still feel overheated somehow
the whole ordeal took perhaps 3 seconds

i trudge through town with my wet jeans clinging to my legs
i do some groceries before i head back to my rented room
what?
i need bread
i leave a tell-tale trail of river-water in the aisles
puddles where i stopped at the chocolate section

when i'm home, my landlord laughs it off like i have
until he says that no one who ever sets foot in that river during winter
comes back out alive
it's too cold
you breathe out when you're really cold
which makes you sink
and if you sink in that river, you're a goner

i tell him my body did the opposite
he looks at me almost without expression
      your body saved you
he says
only now do i realize how close to disaster i was

i am cold for days
paying for the extreme heat of the moment
thank you body
for saving me
yet again

i should honor you with all i have
here
have a whiskey

**seven.**

the unspoken words between a child and a parent
chapters, books, sagas
of pain and love lost in translation
of not knowing how to express the hurt they've caused
the joy they've seen
the person they've become because of the other

what a shame we can never truly explain
whatever a last touch before we part can

**eight.**

every time i think you are leaving my bloodstream
my heart squeezes out an extra pump
and lets you pulsate through my system once more

every time i think; enough!
you have let me down too much
followed through too little
promised me the world and given me a pebble
told me winter tales while
bathing me in sunlight
no wonder i thought we were tropical
no wonder i am lost in this snow

every time that happens i am surprised
by how much it hurts me
how much i love you
how much i miss you
how much i let you live your life without me
i wish i could erase you from my system the way you have erased me
accepted the wonderful year together as passed and
etch-a-sketched a new future
just shake the old reality out
no more you and me
just me
with a trace of you
a fine charcoal line of what was

i don't know
if it makes me a strangely obsessive person
to hold on to what is no longer
or if it makes me a compassionate person
who understands beauty
and doesn't want to give it up

all i know is that i am hurting
and you are not
and i don't want to be

i'm afraid
because the silence, the distance
the compounded miscommunication and selfishness
is causing the sadness to turn wine into vinegar
coleslaw into sauerkraut
peaches into olives
gold to rust

and if you never feel the need to let me know you love me
isn't that almost the same
as not loving me at all?

**nine.**

i feel like i'm shedding so much skin on this journey
i must be becoming a whole new person
only to find it was me underneath all along
just a little shinier
sometimes it's hard to part with the skin you've built
but
gotta love a good peel

**ten.**

i'm dreaming
you're there
you say

> it's just survival
> life is just about survival

i catch you before you slink away
in your plaid short sleeve button-down and beanie

> wait before you go
> i want to say something to you

you shake your head
you already want to exit
but i hold you in place

> you hurt me

i say
i halt
i don't know how to tell you
i wake up a little bit
my awake mind says

> you say it's all about survival
> but part of survival is honest connection
> you're losing an honest connection
> you are not gonna survive this way

i fall back asleep
i meet my friends in a dream i've already had once
friends i don't quite know but are somehow my family
the dream is about the world ending
a force sucked from other dimensions

that is causing the planet to shake and rumble
but we decide to ignore the impending doom
to go see some theatre and eat chocolate

the gulls wake me up
the bed is soft
the day has started
my mind is weary

**eleven.**

"i am enough"
irks me
enough
what is that?
i am so much more

**twelve.**

can i
in the next life
please get
lots of people around me?
is that what i chose for in this one?
to learn how to be alone?

i don't know if i'm learning
i'm just doing
and i'll be alright
my heart is simply aching
all the time

i want family
sisters and brothers
i want big loud dinners
shared toys and bedrooms

i want love
lasting, strong, undoubted love
passionate, beautiful, meant-to-be love
certain, easy, laughter-filled love
i want a family
children of my own to hold and smell and raise
to let into the world where they can hold and smell and raise
to look at my partner and smile with pride and contentment
to know what it is to belong
to connect
to root

this life is an adventure
but it is so detached from everyone

i wonder if in the life filled with people
i would wish to be alone

**thirteen.**

if anything
our past is the sole reason
you should be sharing everything

you came into my heart
as i came into yours
it would be nonsensical
to suddenly cut that part off

right at the moment where you come into joy
and i come into pain
is where people with old bonds thrive
where, when tides turn, we can become the other's buoy

our past is what binds us
not breaks us
after all we've seen within each other
why would we ever become less to one another?

what a damn shame

**fourteen.**

why does it feel like he gets to use something
and i get to lose something?

like he enjoyed my body and i let it be enjoyed?
he can find another body and leave mine in the dust?

can't we have been using each other?
or better yet
can't we have been enjoying each other?

is it because i care and he doesn't?
i get attached and attachment is suffering?
he's able to let each new experience go?
how very buddhist of him

i wish i could either go back in time where i was most important to him
or go to the future where i don't remember him ever being important
instead of this palpitating heart
this aching gut i have to live with now
these questions roving through my brain

**fifteen.**

the sadness and the joy built me into this person
with this voice
and this knowledge
with this understanding
and this embrace

if i didn't have this life
i would have been a different person
not more or less
just different
this is the sabina this life built
and no other

**sixteen.**

i learned today
that beauty is hard to come by
it is an arduous climb
sweaty business
and then to see it is fleeting
and dangerous

this beauty
can be defined by one
adrenaline filled
terrifying moment

the wind whipped me from the side
a giant pushing me out of the way
the path was gouged out of the hill's surface,
and i put one foot against the far side to keep myself upright
     no
i said
teeth gritted
     i win
the mountain and the wind replied in unison and almost blew me
straight off the surface
as easy as a leaf off a tree
i yelled
     fuck you!
     i live!

and it was maybe the first time in a long time where
i fought for my own life
i live
i have things to do

fuck off
there is more

het jaar 2022
the year 2022


a small catalogue of thoughts
on healing and heartache
while traveling


by sabina petra